Mystery Bruise

MYSTERY BRUISE

POEMS BY

TERRY WOLVERTON

Red Hen Press

Los Angeles

Mystery Bruise

Copyright © 1999 by **Terry Wolverton**

ALL RIGHTS RESERVED

No part of this book may be used or reproduced in any manner whatever without the prior written permission of both the publisher and the copyright owner.

Published by
Red Hen Press
P.O. Box 902582
Palmdale, California 93590-2582

Cover design: Susan Silton, S *o* S Los Angeles

Book design by Mark E. Cull

ISBN 1-888996-14-5
Library of Congress Catalog Card Number: 99-63898

• *First Edition* •

Acknowledgments

My heartfelt gratitude goes to Tom Schumacher for his unflagging and generous support, and to Sondra Hale for her commitment and generosity.

These poems were shaped with the wisdom and patience of many individuals, including past and current members of the Women's Poetry Project, especially Megan Black, Ana Castañon, Sheryl Cobb, Yvonne Estrada, Mary Cecille Gee, Robin Podolsky, Kathryn Robyn, Sue Scheibler, and Mary Yarber; members of the Monday night writing group—Jacqueline de Angelis, Julia Gibson, Lynette Prucha-Chavez, and Noelle Sickels; former members of "Live to Write/Write to Live"—Paul Attinello, Gil Cuadros, Kevin Martin, Phil Meyer and Michael Neimoeller; Bia Lowe; and Susan Silton.

Many thanks are extended for the professional courtesies of Robert Drake, John Talbot, Mary-Linn Hughes, and Kate Gale.

Finally, a deep appreciation to my friends, family, students, and caregivers for all of the ways you contribute to my life and work. You make it possible.

Grateful acknowledgment is made to the editors of the following journals in which these poems, or earlier versions of them, first appeared:

Cargo: "Sestina for the End of the Twentieth Century"
The Jacaranda Review: "The Dead Stepfather"
Many Mountains Moving: "We Resist Evolution" and "Legacy"
modern words: "The Sensible Girlfriend"
New American Writing: "Detroit"
The New Press: "Perigee"
Phoebe: "Learning to Lift Weights"
sheila-na-gig: "When We Stopped Being Children" and "Massachusetts"
The Stinging Fly: "In China"
Zyzzyva: "Tubes"

Additionally, "Apocrypha" was commissioned by Project Angel Food; "Legacy" was commissioned as a spoken word piece by the Word L.A. Festival; "Acupuncture" was commissioned by the Los Angeles Festival; and "Supplicant" was published as a bookmark by the MetroArt program of the Metropolitan Transit Authority, Los Angeles, 1997. The title of "broken Water" is taken from the title of an installation by artist Susan Silton.

for ana

Contents

Another mystery bruise   13

I   We Resist Evolution

We Resist Evolution   17
Ants   19
Apocrypha   20
broken Water   22
Perigee   24
September Poem   25
As Vulcan Falls From Heaven   26
Death Sonnets
    Yarzheit   28
    Open Casket   29
    Rite for Julie   30
    Memorial at the Director's Guild   31
    The Dead Stepfather   32
December 26   34
In China   35
The Plum Tree   40
Sestina for the End of the Twentieth Century   41

II   Detroit

Detroit   45
Hymn to a Drinker   49
When We Stopped Being Children   50
The Pink Kitchen   52
Shell   54
Itchy Fingers   56
Waitress   57
The Time Before the Last Time   61
Legacy   65

III *Acupuncture*

Acupuncture	75

IV *Learning to Lift Weights*

Tubes	89
Blues Cruise	92
Shrug	94
The Sensible Girlfriend	96
Massachusetts	98
Musk	100
Learning to Lift Weights	101
Sestina: Sex At Menses	102
Supplicant	104

V *Sink*

Sink	107
New Year	108
Untrust	110
Idolatry	111
Super Lotto	112
to my reluctant valentine	114
Bankrupt	115
Fetish	116
Maria's Lament	118
Body of Work	120
Vampire	122
Poem for My 44th Birthday	123

Another mystery bruise

>blooms above
my knee, the browned purple of a trampled
iris, my legs a garden of abused
blossoms. They sprout like volunteers, rhizomes
set but unremembered under layers
of silt. Flesh bears witness to imperfect
recall: a stab of the lover's elbow
in the crowded tub, somnambulent
collisions with phantom furniture—entire
histories of insult purged from the brain's
slipshod dossier, still recorded with
precision on the derma's faithful log.
Who knows just when these beds were dug, how long
hurt festers before it begins to grow?

I

WE RESIST EVOLUTION

We Resist Evolution

1

I suppose every living thing
resists evolution: the cell that
refuses to split clings in vain
to perfect wholeness; the shapeless blind-
eyed swimmers who did not long to crawl
or breathe, who tried to thwart the limbs and
lungs sprouting up against their will (just
as my breasts did on my childlike
body, and the blood that sprang forth

unbidden like some terrible message
from the future); or the dinosaurs
lumbering the plains when they got
the news they were to be frozen out
of their slice of time. I'm sure they fought
it too, declared apocalypse, deplored
the passing Paleozoic, fierce
as deposed generals and kings, or
deposed lovers forced to build their house

alone. Even at the moment
of death we back away, tread air against
the light that beckons, clutch at our
particular plot of dust. Life is *good,*
we insist, although we know we lie.
Like dinosaurs, we can't imagine
better. It must be coded in our
DNA, this blueprint for reluctance,
rebuffing progress, the unknown.

2

Our tiny planet wobbles in its
orbit, astronauts hum back to us
on satellite beams. Observing Earth,
aquamarine against black velvet;
it makes them want to live forever.
But the atmosphere is choked with warnings
the planet's clock is speeding up, each
moment brings another breakdown,
linkage ruptures, species disappear.

Soon it will be our turn to squall,
take umbrage at our own impending end;
we court nostalgia, pedal backward,
lonesome, suddenly, for all we've known:
picnics, wind-blown maple seeds, the smell
of rain, those early-budding breasts, even
the blood that once mottled our thighs.
It all seems so pleasant now,
as it slips through our wasting fingers.

Inconceivable: that it could just
wink out, another vanishing star;
no one to mourn our absence in the
night. Or that the planet might spin on
without us, its brightest invention.
We won't go down without a fight; armed
with the arrogance of the fittest,
we act like any dying breed, grasp
at a future that resembles now.

Ants

It's as simple as food. Survival: long
black columns of collective mind that stretch
from door to cat's dish, to egg-caked pan left
careless, in the sink.

I'm awed by sheer numbers, no more real to
me than dirt, yet after the massacre—
the flurry of Pine Sol and wet sponges,
wielded with deadly

precision like an assassin's pistol—
some return for their dead. The next morning
a lone speck struggles, black speck corpse on its
back, makes its trembling

way toward home, the unseen nest behind
the backsplash. And I imagine a wake,
tearful creatures upright, front legs lifted
skyward, chanting hymns

as the broken body is laid before
the queen, and I a Hitler, my name cursed,
crimes chronicled, children made to recite
dates of massacres.

Until a friend, someone who in high school
did not skip science class, disrupts my self-
aggrandized guilt: "They retrieve the bodies
not to bury, but

to eat. Practical, not sentimental,
nothing wasted, everything put to use,
which is why their species will survive long
after ours is toast."

Apocrypha

For artists dead of AIDS, a heavenful

Who are these disgruntled angels, their
white robes smirched with streaks of cadmium
or madder, whose withered fists still clutch
at broken stubs of brush or charcoal?
Unlike the other denizens, who've
found contentment in celestial
repose, these restless seraphs stalk
the mist-filled colonnades of heaven,
curse their unseasonable harvest.

One traces air as if to capture
images still teasing at his brain;
another squints as if to frame a
distant square of the horizon, its
properties of shadow and of light.
There's one whose fingers clench and press as
if they ache to mold the firmament,
sculpt and reconfigure the whole star-
strewn plain. And one who strains to arch his

spine once more into an arabesque, or spring
from cloud to cloud in *grand jeté*. There's
one who mutters constantly, tongue still
working words like stubborn clay, but poems
elude like half-remembered music.
Pity these tormented angels. Death
has stolen what they loved best; it's not
the shedding of body, the final
slipping off of that exhausted shell,

nor cherished faces vanishing from
sight. The loss they cannot reconcile
is simply: that *matter*, the raw substance
of art, once bent its will to their
imaginations. Now they hunger
for sensation, crave the smells of ink
and turpentine, the oily slickness
of emulsion, the rough grain of wood,
and the erotic thrall of color,

necessary as food. They scorn this
unrelieved, eternal blue, palette
without darkness or consequence. They
want to play God, the way they used to,
revisioning the world, revealing
what was overlooked. They flex their wings
like pumped muscles, anticipating
flight, as if those downy pinions might
release them from the gates, return them

to their empty studios, where dust
motes swirl in pale beams that pierce through grimy
windows. And we, who still remain,
dwell in the shadows of their absence:
paintings draped in black cloth, stage lights dimmed
like dying stars, the spectrum bleached to
monochrome. "Come back," we implore an
unanswering sky. "Come back, remake
the world for us; restore the radiant

visions, marvelous and strange, that
drained out of our lives the day you left."

broken Water

for Hermine

1

She would never
forget the night
when it all flowed out of her,
this ocean
that had swelled inside her,
billowing, restless waters
swimming with life

and then the final tide,
relentless pull,
the spill.

2

Later,
his friends told her
how he'd done it
in the bathtub;
his young man's
body naked,
immersed, rocking
as the water rose
to claim him,
swaying while his veins—
eager as his mouth
had once sought
comfort at her breast—
sucked milky liquid
from the needle,
its careful dose

how he'd waited
for the tide
to pull him under.

3

Now the sky
beyond the window
is a curve of darkness,
no moon to tug
the surface of the sea;
no matter
how she pours
her teacup empties,
drained of its ocean,

the taste of brine
is always
on her tongue.

Perigee

for Mark

Frost can burn, I think,
and on this night
with the moon too close
I am fevered
in its icy light.

Flames sputter
on the altar set for you.
Caught in a wooden frame,
you clutch your cat,
brown tabby
who now wanders the rooms
searching for your scent.

In the kitchen
I chop rosemary,
slice blood oranges,
my hands stained and fragrant,
feta cheese crumbled
under my fingernails.
These odors
wind around me,
bind me to earth.

I write a message to you
on parchment stamped with gold.
"Watch over us,"
I pray,
then hold the paper
to the flame.
It curls into smoke
and vanishes;
the bright eye of the moon
observes.

September Poem

Summer's end,
the garden's dead,
all liquid sucked
from dirt-dry ground,
the leaves threadbare
on skeletal stems,
the greens replaced
by fading browns.
Already,
light slants overhead,
its shadows wear
away the days,
and what has grown
now blooms no more,
the blossoms sweep
their dusty hems.
Our promises
have long been plucked
and what is left
is all used up;
a dying sun
drops low to mourn
and hears the birds'
exhausted song.

As Vulcan Falls from Heaven

for Paul Monette

Odd, that I should think of Vulcan,
soot-caked deity of toil,
heaven's roughest trade, his brutish
biceps lurid in the fire
light as sweat drops kiss the anvil's
face. Why couldn't I invoke
Apollo, paragon of male
beauty, tender of the Muse? Or
clever Mercury, intrepid
messenger of gods, a mind with

wings? But Vulcan's struck the spark in
my imagination, forged a
chain I can't unlink from you: his
early exile from the hallowed
peaks of Mount Olympus, banished
from the patriarchal kingdom,
judged grotesque, a deviant,
condemned to dwell in half-light, under-
ground. But he did not stay shadowed;
in his crucible he stoked a

blaze that would ignite the world. He
tamed the unrelenting heart of
iron, bent it to his ardor,
fused the fragments of his life and
hammered them to weapons no man
could defeat. The blows rang out like
bells, triumphal notes. Soon all
Olympus came to court his skill; none
could deny his valor, nor his
artistry. There are conflicting

stories of his fall. Some versions
say he was a child when the
pantheon cast him out, declared him
weak, unfit to live with gods. Still
others hold it was because he
challenged the authority of
Jove, who grew enraged and flung the
upstart Vulcan out of heaven. Nine
days and nights he fell, suspended
in the arms of gravity, a

slow and shuddering arc toward the
horizon's rim. With each descending
hour he shone brighter, hurtling
into timelessness, this god of
flame, this blazing nebula. He's
falling still, a fiery streak that
plummets through the sky. Look up and
witness as he passes by: a
trail of spark, a sailing torch; his
burning is a beacon now to
guide us through this unforgiving night.

Death Sonnets

Yahrzeit

for Flora Silton

Your perfume still clings to the bright dresses
that spill from closets; your children clutch silks,
press faces to linen, hungry to breathe
you in. You fill the apartment, shine through
its yellow walls; there's no room you do not
occupy, yet, searching, we cannot find
you, except in dreams. On those nocturnal
visits, you're alive, untouched by tumor;
your lost voice croons, "darling, sweetheart," till we
cleave to sleep, push deeper into pillow,
unwilling to return to this waking
life, your absence, to ignite the candle,
raise a stone to consecrate the wall
between us, living and dead, impregnable.

Open Casket

for Michael

Like all dead bodies, this one bears a pale
resemblance to the living man, the way
a wax apple may be round and red, but
never tempts you to bite. Last night at the
mortuary he looked pretty good, skin
plump as supermarket vegetables,
face almost rosy under the amber
glow of the lamps. Today, in gray church light,
he looks used up, like too-ripe fruit, his lips
bruised blue as early plums. Still, they make us
file past; obedient as children, we
comply. The bravest of us reach to graze
his hands, as if to say good-bye, but it's
too late; the spoiling flesh sags to the touch.

Rite for Julie

Late afternoon sun spills into this white
chapel, pleasant and antiseptic as
the Presbyterians who built it, their
bloodless Christ, their passionless faith, polite

and ever-mindful of appearances.
The pastor's rolling Scottish brogue proclaims
your death at twenty-six not tragedy:
"Her life was full." But these assurances

are pat; it's clear he never met you. No
one acknowledges the singing woman
as your lover, nor we who've gathered as
a chosen family. In this tableau

of empty piety, we're all interred,
our loss compounded, our laments unheard.

Memorial at the Director's Guild

for Paul

A secular temple. Not a detail
of production has been overlooked: stage
cloaked in velvet curtains of dramatic
scarlet, sprays of snowy blossoms circling
the proscenium. In processional,
the Gay Men's Chorus enters, one hundred
strong, sings, "Oh, When the Saints Go Marching In."
Your books are praised; celebrities ascend
the podium, recite your words in grave,
respectful tones. No one forgets their cue
or flubs a line. A seamless spectacle,
standing ovation. We're here to witness
transmutation: the defeated body
is erased, and in its place, myth rises.

The Dead Stepfather

1

You are already dead when I am told
about your fall on New Year's eve, skull cracked
like an egg against Detroit pavement, yolk
seeping into gray matter. How it took
six days to find your next-of-kin, daughter
who said, "Pull the plug."
                              I was your daughter
once; I'm no one now. Thirty-five years since
you brought me red balloons the night you came
to woo my mother, seventeen since we
last spoke. Those years between, a history
of breakage—bones and glass and brittle vows—
the fragile membrane torn, pieces scattered.
No way for me to claim your death; I'm just
the divorced step-daughter, irrelative.

2

If there had been a funeral, incense
would have smelled like gunpowder, gasoline,
and gin, pews crowded with barflys, aging
soldiers, used car salesmen, ghosts of children
clutching red balloons. We would have sung "The
One Rose," in lugubrious chorus, then
shared a stiff drink all around.
                                There was no
service. Three weeks your body stiffened at
the morgue till your daughter found the cheapest
way to burn you, then dispatch your ashes
to a remote grave. Fuck good-byes. In dreams,
I swim with you across a frozen sea,
fathomless blue; we fight the tide, dodge ice
floes white as shells, until you reach the shore.

December 26

It is almost over.
Pack the ornaments
back in their box,
bright bulbs planted in
the dark basement
to await once more
their seasonal appearance.

The calendar
is nearly at its end,
the few remaining pages
transparent as ghosts;
all the lost days and hours
have been plowed under,
compost for memory.

Bury your dead,
their passing marked
in fresh furrows around your mouth.
Your eyes at last tearless,
hollowed to bone,
your tongue has learned
fluency in past tense.

Now the year frays
like a splitting rope
you've been tugging
without gaining ground.
Soon you can let go,
fall back
with a soft thump.

In China

I was already
descending into flu
when I boarded the flight
to Hong Kong,
familiar ache
across my shoulders,
throat raw, throbbing

Tucked in knapsack,
my scribbled greeting
card: "Flying halfway
'round the world for our
anniversary; *that's* how much . . ."
Eight years. Our first
big trip, so long anticipated

Marcus was dying
fungus conquering his lungs
and Gil so sick, wasted
body barely able to contain
his rage; my guilty
phone call from the airport
promised money

for the funeral, all
I could do over staticky
lines, the loudspeaker
garbling my flight
I dragged my baggage
to the metal hull
fifteen hour night

Landed after sunset
of the following day
Hong Kong as fevered
as my own damp skin,
happy anniversary, your
business done, you greeted
me with duty-free perfume

Poême, because I am
a poet, a lavish dinner
I could scarcely swallow,
litany of guidebooks, plans,
all that we would see
I croaked excuses, your eyes
drowned in candlelight

Next day I trudged
with you through fetid
air in clotted
alleyways, climbed
crooked narrow stairs,
laundry flapping thirty
stories up, birds caged

on aerial balconies,
I choked thick
smoke from incense
coils wide as rope
in a red-lit temple.
You were fervid to explore,
I floated underneath

the surface as if
in a dream, drank mango
juice that stung
a swollen throat,
trolled sidewalk stalls,
my temperature soared
until at last, grudgingly

you let me sleep.
On the plane to Beijing
I coughed as if my chest
would fissure, could not
stop, face florid
sputum bloody, you turned
your grimace to the sky

Beijing airport muzak
rendered "Yesterday"
one note and halting, a child's
music box wound down,
relentlessly repeated; endless
yesterday mocked us
all through Customs

In that ancient city,
I stayed in our "deluxe"
hotel, stared through grimy
windows as streams
of cyclists rolled past,
watched Asian MTV,
B-movies while you toured

alone the Great Wall,
the Summer Palace. Was
it here that our hands
began to unclasp?
A week before, I'd walked
Gil through the maze of AIDS
bureaucracy, his voice

raw from screaming
at indifferent clerks,
his fever spiralled, spent
the last of his scant health
to fight for Marcus,
his vow, a good death.
You were furious

I'd come to China
sick, as if infection
were a trick to undermine
your yearning for
adventure. My scorched
cheeks craved your
skinflint touch

I roamed the streets,
lumbering blonde curiosity
swaddled in scarves
spewing tissues like tiny ghosts,
past vendors peddling
Marlboros, the park where
even in dead winter

barbers offer haircuts
until dark, storefronts
heaped with dusty boxes,
unrecognizable—I could
not read the signs
I counted blocks, hunted
landmarks, did not want

to lose you in this city
where I knew no language,
could not count money. Forty
dollar phone call to L.A.,
my American Chinese
doctor told me, "Grief's
exploding in your lungs"

I figured it was Gil,
bereaved, and Marcus,
dead. I couldn't read
the picture alphabet
each character a map
legible as leafless trees
on Beijing winter streets

stark as the scarlet product
of my lungs staining
a white tissue: your dark eyes
turned to distance
scanning an unknown
horizon, both of us
so far from home

The Plum Tree

for Gil Cuadros

Even while dying
the plum tree
bears fruit.
Disease chews
a hole through its trunk,
hollows its core;
bark drops like scales
to dirt.
Even now that I accept
it can't survive,
hard green globes
swing from its branches
to purple and swell
in the sun's glare.

And I think of Gil, who never stopped writing throughout his long season of dying, words burst like blossom from bud, like lesions on the map of his skin, he was made to learn by heart a hundred ways that flesh can fail— lung and nerve, bowel and blood, how the eyes dim, thrush whitens the tongue, intestines surrender

His poems fed on the compost, his decay, grew tart and sweet and swollen as he thinned, he couldn't help it, his nature to bring forth, any more than we could help but pluck a bright plum and bite, its juice stinging our throats

Sestina for the End of the Twentieth Century

As the century slogs to its bloody
conclusion, a culture in death rattles
spits its effluvium, exhausted, parched,
the imagination wound down, a clock,
its heartbeat punctured, dark plasma worn thin—
none of us feeling very well these days.

Paltry and mean, what remains of our days,
the calendar truncated and bloody.
Time is a blade slicing promises thin,
the tick of our hearts worn to a rattle;
faith dissolves beneath the hands of the clock,
prayers beseech a blank sky that remains parched.

Gyrations of love leave us emptied, parched,
its myth too feeble to succor our days.
Sex grinds on, monotonous as a clock,
stained with betrayal, cruel and bloody;
flesh rasps against flesh, dry as a rattle,
the tendons of lust now puny and thin.

Memory too is a garden grown thin,
the soil unwatered, untended seeds parched,
wind whistles through like the ghost of a rattle,
nothing sprouts in the light of these burnt days.
Digging deeper, the spade comes up bloody,
against our wills it unburies the clock.

Sleep is haunted by the leer of a clock,
and even dreams are predictable, thin,
stalked by familiar monsters, bloody
visages that wake us, our clogged throats parched,
swollen with screams unscreamed: another day
of wordless dread, our teeth crazed, rattling.

The vision of future that once rattled
our senses, fueled our race against clock,
has collapsed into a stretch of lost days;
lesioned tomorrow, its bones whittled thin,
beckons a skeletal hand, and the parched
tear ducts squeeze out a last few drops of blood.

Unimagined days, measured like a clock's
last breath, played on a parched stage; a ratty,
thin curtain descends, the color of blood.

II

Detroit

Detroit

Alone and
speeding
through the dark,
driving, of course—
it's Detroit
where nothing exists
but roads,
blacktop slicing landscape
like spokes of a wheel,
fanning out
from the city's
pustulant heart,
even the freeways
walled in concrete
lest a scrap
of scenery
tear your eye
from the pavement
swallowed beneath.

It's been years
since the years
I drove these
wide-laned boulevards,
endless nights,
west to east
then hurtling north
like a bird
at winter's end,
some genetic imperative
guiding my navigation,
only the radio
for company,
rock and roll
rhythm and blues
shriek of jazz

all a Detroit girl
could ever need,
and whispers of smoke
climbing the air
from bright ends
of joints,
like tiny gems
or stars,
smoke sucked in
like oxygen,
foot to the pedal,
streetlights
one long smear
of white,
night through
an open window,
impossible to stop.
Years since
those road signs
seared my retina,
their alphabets
reflecting
in my headlights—
Gratiot, Woodward,
Greenfield, Livernois—
learning them by heart;
they were black mysterious rivers,
banks lined with
boarded-up buildings,
dim, faltering neon,
and farther north,
broad dark lawns
of the suburbs,
silent as death.
But I was alive,
streaking past

in my screaming steel hull,
wheels spinning
like shiny coins,
and the music inside
wailed a jittery beat,
no thought of destination,
as long as
I could travel
these black waters,
these inky ribbons of road,
as long as my headlights
shone forward.

Now those years
are left,
like this city,
in dust,
viewed only
through a rearview mirror,
and I return
to drive these roads
as if something
could be reassembled,
a piecing together
of shards,
but new thoroughfares
have been carved,
the old ones
are paved over,
layers of asphalt
burned into my skin,
my mouth full
of gravel and tar,
whole blocks of buildings
have been razed,
lots glitter

with exploded glass,
and the road signs
gleam with
a thin membrane
of recognition,
each shining letter
a code for memory,
maps dissolve,
radio
throws up
static,
and each road avoids
the scarred heart
of city,
agreeing only
to circle its perimeters,
wary and slit-eyed,
beast
that stalks
its prey.

Hymn to a Drinker

Sacred, the rituals of ice splintering
under that first splash of fluid,
this nightly baptism: cubes bob
in their sodden universe, then
surrender their form. Like a saint
you've sacrificed earthly
attachments: battered black

Cadillac, chubby daughter who waits
in the pink kitchen, counting
sins on the ticks of the clock.
You remain devoted to a god
who delivers you from broken
promises, blurs the face
in the mirror, mutes hurled curses.

Holy, the way you've suspended
your life in the clear blood of grain,
the way days float and spin
in that swirling world, how
you swallow each drop until time
is drained and the empty
glass brims again.

When we stopped being children

Raggedy Ann has cancer.
She slumps
on the shelf
at the back of the dark closet,
beige skin yellowed,
stained and splitting,
soft white insides
swelling, spilling out,
the cottony squish of them.

She's been there
since the day
Daddy broke her,
bit that secret heart
beneath her dress,
etched those words
"I love you"
into scars
upon her flesh.

Now a halo of red dust
covers her
as her yarn hair
frays and thins;
a button has popped
where an eye once was,
underneath, a dot,
pink as her youth,
but it sees nothing at all.

Her clothes hang loose
on her slackening form,
apron greying,
bloomers slid
to the ankles' curve;
her hidden heart
all but forgotten,
painted smile
fades to brown.

The Pink Kitchen

After school I'd blast the radio
to fill the empty rooms—
"Goin' To A'Go-Go" and "Tears of a Clown"—
stuffing white bread, Cheez-Whiz,
and A-1 Steak Sauce sandwiches
into pudgy cheeks. Daylight
slipped from the sky while I'd empty
brimming ashtrays, rinse
sticky glasses still sour
with last night's gin.

The white dishwasher floated
in the middle of the room
and I'd load yolk caked
plates, lipstick rimmed cups
and blackened pans, then roll
its metal carcass to the sink, attach
black tubes to faucets like life support.
Motor hum and churning water drowned
the music, and the air would smell
of harsh soap and hot rubber.

When the cycle ended, my body
no longer thrumming with noise,
the house would be lonelier,
windows dark, radio now muted
by the clock's nervous heartbeat,
dishes too hot to touch.
Black phone hung smug on the wall,
it could taunt with silence or with lies,
my mother's promises wormed
through tangled cord: she'd be home

soon. Behind her would be sounds
of crowds and neon, glasses clinking
smoke rising in dim light. But I lived
in the pink kitchen, stared into cabinets
of Lipton, Campbell's, Minute Rice,
awaiting headlights in the drive.
Butter would be always melting
in its dish on the wood-grain table,
cubed edges softening, yellow
darkening to gold.

Shell

I could have anything I wanted
from the maws of the vending machines
that stood watch over the waiting
room of my stepfather's Shell station.
Larry or Chubbs would fish out keys
with grimy fingers, swing open
the face of the machine, reveal its innards
stacked columns of soda or candy bars.

Outside the constant ding of the bell
as cars pulled in for gas, directions,
air in the tires, a clean windshield,
drivers impatient for destination,
and Chubbs or Larry would dash, leave
me to choose: Planter's Peanut
Bar or Nestle's Crunch, Coke
or orange or chocolate pop. Grit

covered that tiny room, layered
on maps in their laddered racks, dusting
the globe of the gumball machine,
sifted over neat rows of motor oil
in silver cans, smudging the white
pages of homework I filled with
painstaking script. I breathed
the stink of petroleum, kicked

at the legs of a yellow plastic
chair with my black and white
school oxfords, waiting for my stepfather
who was supposed to watch me till
my mother got off work. Nine was too
young, she thought, to stay at home alone.
But every day he'd disappear, banged-up
Chevy gone from the lot, the men

in oil-streaked uniforms shrugging excuses.
"Anything she wants," he'd instructed them,
and I watched the clock as the sky
darkened and the bright shell glowed
against night. My new bra was too tight;
I hugged my three-ring binder to hide my roll
of belly from Larry, from Chubbs, and sucked
the dregs of chocolate pop or lemon-lime.

Itchy Fingers

Shoplifting is a sleight-of-hand;
cartsful of merchandise disappear like doves into a woolen coat sleeve.
Security cameras overlook the overweight girl in pink glasses.
Though sweat sprouts on skin beneath winter layers,
you question the sales clerks, bold, "Do you have that single, 'Itchycoo Park'?"
and test the perfumes, spritzing a thick cloud of Emeraud,
sit at the lunch counter, crunching Coke-flavored ice between molars.
Though the pulse shudders like the roar from a freeway overpass,
you stay cool, the Bonnie Parker of Grandland Shopping Center.

But it's not magic that's at work here, just nerve.
Behind the good-girl-good-grades-speaks-respectfully-to-teachers
lurks one who spits on the rules,
whose blood runs black as a gas pump,
and the five-finger discount is nothing less than you deserve,
because Dad walks around in his boxers, crotch gaping.

Scraps of notebook paper scrawled in science class:
"Yardley lip gloss, Petals O'Pink" and "Panty-hose, size small, dark tan,"
florid evidence of new-found friends
who feed like parasites on your risk-taking.
The skilled thief makes herself invisible, like she's learned at home,
evaporating just before the fights start, the amazing Wolverine.

And even after being caught and caught again,
after the black police car, no handles on the doors inside,
a long wait in the barred, beige room, after the telephone line
has snapped and Dad's battered your jaw with the deafened receiver,
after the judge, the juvenile psychiatrist, three months' grounding,
you will keep stealing.

You steal because your hands are so strong and empty.
Carpe diem.
Your digits itch, blood burns with the stink of gasoline.

Waitress

I had
all the requirements
to do this job:
strong legs,
sure wrists,
a deep desire
to please.

More coffee?
Would you like that
toasted?
How 'bout
a little ice cream
on that pie?

I had a
dull gold uniform
in a Colonial style,
my size
or two sizes larger,
whatever came
in the laundry,
an apron
stretched across my hips,
white shoes
scuffed grey
beneath their
nightly coats of polish.
Still I had my vanity:
my tresses brushcut
to elude
the dreaded hairnet.

I had
one hundred hands
to carry steaming platters
on scarred aluminum trays,
to ladle greasy dressings
onto mounds of lettuce,
and sweep the coins
into my bottomless
pockets.
I had a smile
for every customer—
the screaming child
the pouty shopper,
the regular, the lech,
the finicky dieter,
the ones who never tipped.
They all called me
"Waitress."

I had dreams
like crumpled napkins,
desire caked like
egg yolk on a plate.
I was twenty,
college drop-out,
and the future simmered
lukewarm
on the burner
with the daily special.

I had
a glow in my brain
from the dope
I smoked
every morning
on the drive in,

Led Zeppelin
on the radio
cranked louder
than my thoughts;
I had a pliable spine
from the Valium
gulped with my
first cup of coffee.
I had coffee all day long,
cup after cup after cup;
dark sludge
kept the edge
in my brain.
I had a joint
in my pocket
for the slow stretch
of late afternoon,
sometimes shared
with the busboys
in the dishroom,
behind the long conveyer,
and for breaks,
a nearby bar,
where the coins
in my pocket
bought whisky sour,
tequila sunrise,
slo gin fizz
until the clock struck five.

After,
I returned to my station,
cleaned mayonaise
from under my fingernails,
spritzed Binaca
through rubbery lips.

I had
a new pad of checks
in my pocket,
drawers full of
knives, forks, spoons,
still hot
from the dishwasher's maw.
I had
four hours to go,
thirty-six
chairs to fill,
and each night I turned
to face the dinner rush,
my metal tray
before me
like a shield.

The Time Before the Last Time

July breaks open
like a blister.
Heat enfolds you,
hands clasped
in a desperate prayer.
Wear a gauzy dress
into the coffee shop

while hard-eyed lesbians
sneer behind
plates of ham and eggs,
pools of butter
congealing on cold toast.
Slink home to your attic
rooms, where mice

run through the walls,
and the dough-faced guy
at the bottom of the stairs
masturbates all day long
in the open door.
Lie on the same narrow bed
you slept in as a child; watch

the eaves loom closer.
A window opens into sky,
but the leaves remain mute.
Wander to the kitchen;
your refrigerator harbors
only cheap red wine,
a half-eaten carton of yogurt,

the freezer frosted shut.
The pills gleam in your palm
like lodestars, falling
one by one into your dark
universe, washed down with
the last drop of burgundy.
Leave the empty bottles

on the kitchen sink
and make a call.
It's not that you want your friend
to leave her job
at the Chinese restaurant,
put down her grease-stained apron,
peddle home on her bicycle

to stop you. You just want her
to look after your cat.
Later, awaken in a trailer,
wind rattling the flimsy walls,
a former lover by your side.
She no longer loves you.
Still, she was the one

to tell the E.R. staff
it was an accident,
so you wouldn't be locked up.
This morning, you aren't grateful.
Remember that this woman keeps a gun
—she once took you shooting,
tin cans through the heart—

and, cunning, begin to search.
Find instead the razor
but it won't cut deep enough.
Demand, at last, to leave until,
exhausted, the woman
who no longer loves you agrees.
Drive unsteadily, pills

still orbiting like comets
in the bloodstream,
drive to the softball field,
still in your gauzy dress,
now streaked with red;
cross the diamond while
tight-shouldered lesbians

stop the game and stare.
Drift home again to the musty
attic, stagger up the stairs;
the dough-faced fondler eyes you with
disgust. Your hand-
washed pantyhose still hang
in the tiny bathroom

beside the pressed uniform.
Spoon some cat food;
bandage your wrists. Meteors whirl
before your eyes till night succumbs.
Tell your boss you scraped
your arms sliding into first base;
coffee cups rattle in your hands,

your smile crooked as you
serve the customers
tossed salads and pot pies.
For eighteen days after, eat nothing,
black coffee and grapefruit juice;
your body grows thin as a boy's.
Strain to remember

those nineteen hours
when oblivion swallowed you,
only to spit you out.
It will be years before you are grateful,
weeks till your ears stop ringing,
till the pills are purged from your system,
comets that burn themselves out.

Legacy

I was twelve years old
when I watched the tanks
advance up Grand River Avenue,
lumbering as dinosaurs,
or squat, giant insects,
their khaki camouflage
conspicuous
against gray Detroit streets.
1967.
That was the summer
my stepfather left our home
to move in with his girlfriend,
a temporary cease-fire
in the nightly battle
of our living room.
That summer
my mother and I
lived alone,
and she became
as thin as bone;
retreating
to a bottle of gin,
she nursed her grief.
She feared the fires
that bloomed miles
from our neighborhood,
feared
the dark-skinned people
shown scuffling with police
on TV screens,
the neighbors' desperate rumors
that saw chaos moving closer,
ever closer
to our home.

I was twelve years old
and already
split in two,
confined to my home,
to my neighborhood,
confined in my traitorous skin,
but something in me
was burning too,
hot as the flames
devouring
the clapboard homes
of Twelfth Street;
something had been ignited,
and when the neighbors scoffed,
"It's so senseless,
torching
their own neighborhoods;
they're just
making it worse
for themselves,"
I did not agree.
I was only twelve,
but I already knew
the way some kinds of pain
can only be relieved by fire.

Twelve years old.
Split in two
and split again,
combustion inside
stretched white paper skin.
I wished they
would come to my neighborhood,
I wanted them
to burn it to the ground,
and I

would help them.
But
I was afraid.
Afraid that they
would never see
the flames that flared
inside of me,
that they would never
see beyond
the white bone cage
of history
that bound me
to that place.

1968.
I was thirteen
and I learned my name,
I walked the corridors
of junior high,
that blasted, unrecovered city,
walked the halls
and learned my name
that day in 1968,
a knot of bodies
in the corridor
clustered 'round a radio,
a knot of bodies,
forbidden radio,
1968,
my junior high.
The announcer was reporting:
Martin Luther King
was dead,
crumpled on a balcony
in Memphis,
dead,

and the knot of bodies
twisted, wrenched,
the flames inside me
beat like wings
like whips,
it stung,
it opened me,
and I was pulled
by strands of grief
and strands of disbelief,
pulled by flame,
I learned my name,
the knot snarled:
White. Bitch.
Get. Away. White. Bitch.
I learned my shame.

1968.
I was thirteen.
My stepfather
lived with us
once again;
the war resumed,
there was gunshot
in the living room.
My stepfather
reeked of gasoline.
Armies of dark people
stalked his dreams,
invading our living room,
stealing his TV.
Night after night
he waited for them,
crouched
by the empty window,
his hand

on the trigger.
He believed
they'd come
to take from him
his plunder,
all that he had wrested
from this life:
his war-hero history,
his alcoholic dreams,
his ruined stepdaughter.
He muttered,
uttered curses,
warned me of
the danger of
dark men to young white girls.
But whatever could they
do to me
that he had not
already done?
His fingers
on my breasts,
his soft, insinuating voice,
his red dick
swollen in my hands.
Gunshot
in the living room.
Gunshot
everywhere.

1971.
I was sixteen.
Gunshot.
On the other side of town
my friend Greg
was killed while sleeping,
his face dark

against the pillow,
caught a bullet
in his brain,
blood shot like flame.
Shot by some
white father/war-hero,
determined to defend
his daughter
from his nightmares.
Gunshot.
My friend Greg,
wasn't sleeping with
the daughter,
only sleeping,
on a cot
in the same room,
their rainbow commune.
Gunshot.
The father
killed his daughter too,
killed everybody
sleeping in that room.
And my step-father
flashed his gun,
swore that he would kill me
if I dared to mourn.
The funeral was crowded;
I was late and rain-soaked
as I slunk into a pew.
Surrounded by
Greg's family,
I felt ashamed.
I was sure
that they would
know my name.
I was sure

that they would
see in me
the white bone cage
of history,
sure that they
would see the one
who'd put a bullet
in their son.
Get. Away. White. Bitch.
A stitch of fear
ran through my blood,
but what they saw
with their uncluttered vision,
their eyes of tears,
was just a girl,
rain-drenched and trembling,
pale as sleet,
a member of
the family
of grief.

1992.
I am
thirty-eight years old.
Trash swirls past
the vacant lots
on Grand River Avenue,
but I have left
those streets behind,
blown across the continent
to this ravaged city
of Los Angeles;
it is my home.
The gash, the split
has never knit together—
a white woman

in a Third World city,
I am flames inside
a cage of bone,
a dinosaur
on this turning wheel.
1992.
It is April
on an L.A. freeway.
I am speeding
in the coffin of my car
along this graveyard.
I am thinking
about none of this,
I am empty of history,
empty of flame,
I have no name.
And then the radio
brings the news.
My eyes craze
like shattered marbles,
a ripple of fire
erupts
at the base of my spine.
Not. Not. Not. Not.
Guilty.
I fall through time.

III

Acupuncture

Acupuncture

"In order to bring into harmony the human body one takes as standard the laws of the four seasons and the Five Elements."

—Nei Ching: The Yellow Emperor's
Classic of Internal Medicine

for Dr. Ellen

The needles
quiver slightly,
rising out of my skin
like flags
planted in the crust
of a conquered moon,
slender metal spires
poked into dermis,
conducting current
through tissue
like power lines
buried underground.

I am lying
on my back.
Needles sprout
from hands and feet,
shoot skyward
from scattered points
on my belly,
along the breast bone;
a single spike
pierces my third eye.
I imagine myself
in aerial view:

a thumb-tacked map
of a region at war,
pins to signify
places where
fighting's broken out.

I have come
to this white room
with a litany
of complaint:
fatigue
and headaches,
my face erupted,
weeping eczema
that blisters my fingers,
spear that stabs
my abdomen
each time I eat,
breasts that swell
and ache
like bloated flowers
before each menstrual purge,
an inability
to breathe.

My doctor calls it
"peeling the onion,"
the way we must go
layer by layer,
delving
like geologists
through strata
until we reach
the core, origin
of all this malady.

My doctor—
an American Jewish lesbian
practicing
Traditional Chinese Medicine—
lifts my wrists
to feel my pulses,
her fingers know
the vast percussion
of the body;
each organ
plays a different tempo
and she scans
its prosody.
She studies
my extended tongue;
it trembles,
stretched beyond
the dark cave
of my mouth,
like a mole
that stumbles,
blinking,
for the first time,
into light.
So much there is
to be unearthed.

For her
the body is
no mere lump
of viscera,
no simple machine
with replaceable parts—
organs, pumps, drainage—
no product of
the Industrial Revolution.

For her
the body is
a network of pathways,
along which
energies fly
like cars at night;
and those
illuminated highways
link the territories of
corpus, brain and spirit;
realms long severed
are revealed to be
inseparable as metaphor.

For her the body
is like shale,
history compressed
into layers,
the silt-strewn
record of the life.

The outer layer
wears the bruise
of everyday behavior:
the imprint
of Los Angeles,
its petrochemical air,
a mordant tang
to drinking water,
relentless thrum
of electromagnetic waves
plucking our nerves
like a frenzied bassist.
Years of
eighty-hour work weeks,
bound to the calendar page

like a silent movie heroine
roped to railroad tracks,
train always pressing down.
The lengths to which one goes
in order not to feel.
They call it "stress,"
slow grinding
of tectonic plates;
what once was solid,
now broken,
layer against layer,
a gradual puckering,
and then rupture,
sudden slam,
fissuring of sleep.

Before this,
there were other excesses.
The child
who sought solace
in Sweet Tarts,
Milk Duds,
M&Ms,
Butterfingers,
Hershey's kisses,
malted milk balls,
hot fudge sundaes,
Pecan Sandies,
jelly doughnuts,
Bun Bars and after dinner mints,
Toll House cookies,
Turkish Taffey,
Heath Bars and
German chocolate cake
became
the adolescent drinker:
martinis blended

from the family stash
before the junior high school dance;
sweet wine
passed hand to hand
in the high school basement.
Bass Ale chased
tequila shooters
in the bar just off campus,
where I—fledgling feminist—
proved that I could
drink as much
as any man.
There was white rum
for seducing the first woman,
Pernod or Ouzo
in the lesbian bars,
Burgundy to pass
lonely summer afternoons
and honey-colored scotch
at night.

Even this
was not enough.
I was fashioning
a chain-link fence,
an Iron Curtain,
my own private Cold War
waged with chemistry:
caffeine and cocaine,
opium and mescaline,
Quaalude and Tuinal,
hashish and angel dust,
tetrahydrolcannabinol,
lysergic acid diethylamide.
Daily were
the ramparts
fortified.

And leering
on the other side
of this elaborate barricade
are children,
monstrous and grotesque,
their fingers
pecking at the mesh
like birds of prey.
Each wears my face:
the mewling infant
purpled by
her daddy's fists;
the five-year-old,
hands sticky with
the semen
of her stepfather;
the pudgy
girl of nine, alone,
in the dark house,
pacing,
talking to herself,
as clock hands
crawl toward midnight.

There's one child
who's as good
as death,
frozen, pale,
scared to breathe,
another one
who wields an ax,
her hair and clothes
a shit-streaked mess,
black blood
spills from her tongue.
They huddle like refugees,

howl and whine
and undermine the parapet,
worm through the chinks
to suck the breath
that curls from my lips.

Partitions crumble,
floors collapse
and leave us
swaying at the brink;
below our listing feet
there roils the rancid stew
from which we sprang,
its wretched recipe
passed on,
a message
coded in the cells,
its foul ingredients
fed to us
before the zygote
gathered form.
This bitter brew,
this legacy,
it welters, molten,
at the core.

This, then,
is how deep
the probe must go.

My doctor
draws a diagram,
a scraggly
five-pointed star,
to show the wheel

of elements,
the weddedness of all
life's matter:
water
nourishes wood,
wood yields
to fire,
fire's residues
feed the earth;
from the earth's core
metal is exhumed,
and metal
gives its minerals
to water.
So the wheel turns.

What poet
could resist
this medicine,
where everything
is metaphor
and systems parallel:
diagnosed with
earth imbalance,
I know that
it's from years
of trying to find
safe ground,
unpoisoned soil
in which to
set roots down,
when thought alone
was bedrock,
and I buried
every dangerous feeling
beneath the loam of reason.

Too much earth
becomes obsession,
compresses into rock;
the will stretches
like a tree branch
or a wand
until its reaches are exhausted
and it snaps:
liver set against spleen,
two snarling warriors,
circling.

And still,
beneath this layer
lurks one more:
the realm of water,
sickly gruel of fear
in which I floated
in my amniotic prison;
deficient water,
dread of immersion,
an inability to float,
a distrust
of deep seas
that finds me
scrabbling
on the desert floor,
itself once ocean,
now fissured, parched
fluidity rejected,
thirst renounced.

Evolution
in reverse;
I must crawl back,
on disappearing limbs,

and scrape my belly
against the moistening sand
to drink beside
the undulating hem
of water;
slip in,
slip in,
till my head
fills with its roar:
here is the spirit
that must finally
be restored.

IV

LEARNING TO LIFT WEIGHTS

Tubes

There's one called "Wild,"
weird coppery purple
I wore when I first
went blonde, my early
thirties. Wax cylinder
now worn to the rim
of its metal casing,
convex bed of color
I can only scrape out
with a fingernail, but
no one makes this shade
anymore, so I keep it.

"Exactly Red"—same
vintage: mid-1980s,
when platinum and scarlet
accessorized a black
slip and spiked heels.
It's "featherproof,"
guaranteed not to bleed
beyond the lips'
outline into cracks
that sprout like tributaries
from my mouth more
than a decade later.

"Odyssey," the dull plum
bought after I became
a redhead, worn for everyday,
almost a neutral. "Midnight,"
a stain, purchased to replace
the discontinued "Blackberry."
"Media," blood red so dark
it's nearly black (should
have been called "Medea"),
worn with a 90s

snarl, and never
without lipliner,

but too dark for the blonde
I again assumed, hair shirred
to scalp, bleached raw to cheer
myself after my lover's mother
died of cancer. The current crop
includes three purples: "Lust,"
a frosted lavender too
young for me, but I like
how it transports me
to the 60s, my teens,
to Yardley and Carnaby Street,
to Love perfume;

"Grid," blue-violet as
metallic as a shield;
and "Epic," a rich grape
about which a stranger
in the checkout line
of the health food store
said to me, *If you're going
to wear purple lipstick,
you better have a sense
of humor.* And I suppose
I do—my face the canvas
of a would-be Dadaist,

never destined for greatness
so all the more willing
to risk. *If you can't be
beautiful, look interesting*—
the motto I've upheld since
fifth grade when I used
my Christmas money

for my first tube, no demure
pink for this ten-year-old,
but "Cherries in the Snow,"
like my mother wore, bright
cerise too old for me.

Even the mistakes amuse:
"Cadeaux," a harsh magenta,
or my Lancome gift-with-purchase,
"Rouge Essential"—let's just say
some people weren't born
to wear orange. And recently
"Mint Sorbet," the pale green
frost I chose at Thrifty's
in the desert, the one
that turns to peach and then
sloughs off in flakes after
a few hours. When people

tell me *Everytime I see you,
you look different.
I didn't even recognize you*
I grin through lips that might
be flushed with "Dubonnet"
or cooled with "Opaline."
That's the beauty of it:
by day I'm "Hyper,"
by night a "Siren,"
and essence
bows to
mutability.

Blues Cruise

Los Angeles Harbor is choked
with garbage. Clumps of styrofoam
cling to the hull of the Hornblower;
we stand in line to board. Captain
greets us, fake brass and heartiness;
corporate sponsors hand out free
packs of cigarettes. We hand ours back.

The ship is crowded with couples
dressed for a musical moonlit
cruise along the industrial
shoreline. Men grasp women's arms
with proprietary ease; we
are the only ones without male
escorts: jean jacket / leather jacket.

Dinner has been promised so we
quarrel with a uniform about
an empty table on the upper deck;
"Reserved," he sniffs, and gestures
toward the dock: a bride—resplendent
Cinderella in pink satin—
her long train a blushing serpent
inching up the gangplank.

The teenaged bride is trailed by
her groom, surf-tanned, thin and callow
in his tux, sun-kissed South Bay kids,
their doting families. The blues
enthusiasts make way for them
and watch, misty with nostalgia
or regret. You reach to clutch my hand.

As the ship churns from shore, the sea
is swallowing the last daylight.
The bands begin to play. Old Black

men pick and pluck and wail while our
newlyweds dance an awkward two-
step; the crowd whistles and applauds.
We turn our backs, scan ragged skyline.

We search three decks in vain for others
like us, dance together anyway,
fast songs, then—with courage—slow;
I slide my hipbones under yours,
sway to the low sobs of the bass
and, insistent, wind my arms tight
around your neck, despite the stares.

Later some friend asks, "Why would you
go?" And I say, because we love
the blues, because we have a need
to dance. I've learned to shield my scarred
eyes from the searing gaze of
disapproving strangers, earned the right
to sway with the rhythm of the sea.

We dock at midnight, start the long
trudge to our parked car, pass the pink-
clad bride dissolved in tears. We hear
a woman scream and race to help
but Security gets there first;
when we catch up, the groom's restrained,
still thrashing in the guard's strong grip.

He's trying to ram his head against
chainlink; a frantic bridemaid in
her ruined gown begs, "Don't hurt him,
he's on drugs." We don't stay to hear
the final bars of this tired song;
my cheek rests on your thigh the whole
way home, the blues still echoing.

Shrug

"All lesbians have tight shoulders,"
a burly woman told me, my second time
in a dyke bar. We were leaning
on the jukebox, our features flushed
in crimson light. She reached to squeeze
at my constricted muscles, nodded approval.

Today I think of her, how she'd approve
the unyielding formation of my shoulders,
while a masseuse prods and squeezes
at their stubborn knots. Twenty years' time
gone, yet granite underneath the flesh
remains, a rock to lean on.

The diligent masseuse is gentle. She leans
into the fiber, tenderly reproving
the resistant tissue, coaxing. She applies fresh
oil that smells of sage, as if these guarded shoulders
might yet be disarmed. She works overtime
but when I leave, my left trapezius is still squeezed

and aching. My car re-joins the squeeze
of traffic on the freeway; I press the pedal, lean
into the steering wheel, late now, fretting time,
as if my sweat and curses could improve
the drive. This tension lodges in my shoulders,
the muscles cramp, a stab of pain flashes

through my neck. But isn't this a symptom of a life flush
with vigor, a commitment to squeezing
every drop from every day, of shouldering
responsibility for satisfaction, leaning
toward excess instead of scarcity? Who can prove
this has to do with lesbianism, and not the times

in which we live? And yes, of course, the times
are hostile to us, our appetites reviled, flesh
despised, our couplings denied approval,
our very sense of self squeezed
into constricted definitions, narrow lines.
All this rests upon our shoulders,

and over time, its weight compresses, squeezes
until we're either crushed or hardened, rawboned and lean,
defiant of approval and fortified with steel shoulders.

The Sensible Girlfriend

for C.

Like shoes
she chose for comfort,
not for style,
that fit her contours
without chafe
or blistering

Here is sanity.
It took her years to arrive,
like an explorer
settling at last
into uneasy retirement,
a small cottage
at the edge of the sea.
How the breakers crash
against the underpinnings;
still, the walls hold firm.
Hearth blazing steadily,
she tries to warm to it

tells herself
she is mature now,
this is good.
The days of stalking,
done,
the rabid pulse,
the blood-drenched kisses,
all behind her now.
Wearied, finally,
of careless cruelties,
she will stay here,
grow old

with you.
And, sensible,
lacking her gift
for self-deception,
you know she struggles
with devotion,
you listen as she
moans inside her dreams,
and watch, without remarking,
as she tracks the tap of high heels
just beyond the window,
their rhythm growing fainter
with each step.

Massachusetts

We fought in Salem,
as she nosed the rented car
through streets that
stubbornly refused to match
the squiggled lines
accordioning from my lap.
She pressed me for direction
as I spun the folding paper
like a compass point,
urged me for instruction
as I traced the lines like braille,
my fingers blinded,
tapping out the spell of history;
I could not navigate this town.

How could I explain
the pall of Salem?
There's not an inch on Earth
that isn't steeped in blood—
corpses pushing up the cobblestones
in every town,
and the buildings that blunt the sky
are girdered in bone.
One could travel anywhere
and feel that chill,
the hovering of ghosts
above the landscape,
the past's damp breath
against the ear.

This town, though,
descended like a shroud
upon my holiday;
Salem,
its rectilinearity
compressed the ribbon of my spine
and sealed my thighs
like doorways to a crypt;
Salem,
its somber abnegation,
grimmest reprobation
sought to suck me to a hollow shell
through which the vengeful cries of God
then could be heard.

My lover, steering wheel in hand,
stared into narrow streets
with the eyes of a dark bird.
"Which way," she cawed, "which way?"
But mine glowed with the blankness
of a woman swaying from a noose,
clothing asunder,
curses drowning in an airless throat,
spirit driven from its home;
it circled now above our heads.
The useless atlas crumpled at my feet,
it could not lead me to a place
where threat did not bear down like heavy stones;
we fought in Salem.

Musk

You slathered musk
oil over your neck
and shoulders, under
your arms, along
the length of your thighs,
leaving its residue
on everything you touched,
aura splayed in rooms
you moved through
resonant with thick
perfume, scent squeezed
from glands of male
deer or civet, lingering
for hours like the memory
of a kiss; I grew reluctant
to kiss, knowing I'd reek
the remainder of the day,
fearing to lose my own
essence, become unrecognizable
to my senses; you were
vying for air space,
marking territory,
crowding me out
and near the end you
looked at me, stricken,
accusing, "You don't even
like the way I smell."

Learning to Lift Weights

1

At first, you've no idea what you can do;
your arms, soft as bread dough and without shape,
seem cowed by even the simplest task,
shuddering, straining underneath the weight
of a slender bar; your legs, thick, dumb stumps,
inarticulate as iron; heart made
swollen with forced blood. Always you must lift
against the doubt, your mother's voice replayed
in fearful cadences, the endless loop
inside your head, you underestimate
your strength, cannot imagine power that
does not bring punishment. Still, how you hate
your weakness; when at last the bar does rise
buoyed by your newfound muscles, celebrate.

2

By now you know the way the cells respond
to injury, the damage you inflict;
you tear them down to build them doubly strong,
a discipline both rigorous and strict.
Just like your father, military man
who wielded weapons: his thundering fists,
his blasting words, his violating hands
exploded in you, taught you to resist.
The cells dilate and toughen with each stress;
and now, no matter how they load the bar,
your face remains impassive as you press
iron to heaven, reshaping who you are
despite the pain, the inner bleeding, a
pitiless God who molds his lumps of clay.

Sestina: Sex at Menses

There was a time when this exchange of blood
seemed sexy, dangerous and flouting
the taboos of mothers and the queasy phobias
of men. Defiantly we'd streak our thighs
with crimson, fingers dipped and dripping
while the scarlet Rorschach spread along the sheet.

The body's calendar, its well-thumbed sheets
demarking the expected time of blood,
could not disrupt our hungers, the dripping
of desire, a pulse, pure, insistent. Flouting
the etiquette of Kotex advertising, our thighs
opened, arching, mocking patriarchal phobias

of women, our stain, our sex unclean, the phobia
of witches, our hidden power, the inscribed sheet
of our crimes. We'd cackle, diving between spread thighs
to feast, our lips crowned with blood,
salt-sweet on our tongues, fluting
the soft crenelations dripping,

one fluid melting into another, viscous, dripping
deep into the reptile brain, rooting past phobias,
beyond all civilizing influence, flaunting
our animal selves, the sheets
become earth, become mud wallows, sticky with blood
coating our torsos, legs and thighs.

But now we are more circumspect. Our thighs,
no longer firm, ravaged by years that drip
through a sieve of time, our blood
more sour, sharper, fuel for new phobias
of aging. Rigid on the stretched sheet
we know no longer how to flout

the culture that is rooted in us. Or how to flout
the virus, deadly spectre that threatens to invade our thighs.
Our passion, when it sparks at all, glimmers behind sheets
of latex, its taste industrial and flat. We staunch the dripping
of our fluids, avoiding touch, our bodies phobic
to us now. The memory of our rituals of blood

fades, even as blood fades, as our youthful flouting
of men's laws fades, leaving phobias intact and thighs
sealed. Our revolution dribbles through our fingers, stains this sheet.

Supplicant

An angel waits by the side of the road.
I glimpse her first at a distance, something
gleaming up ahead, the way slanting sun
strikes a pane of window, brightness at the
periphery of sight. Coming nearer
I see form: a stately posture, swirling
gown, an arc of wings. I assume that she
has come to help me, and I am relieved.
If senseless utterings in the dark can
be called prayers, then I have prayed for this. Some
blessed wisdom, respite. Then I see her
eyes. White-blue, a frozen lake, terrified.
Her wings sooty, trembling with dread; she kneels
on broken asphalt and implores, "Save me."

V

Sink

Sink

Can't wash that glass
with your lip print—
swath of cerise
on pale green glass—
perched at the edge
of my kitchen sink

It greets me this
morning like a kiss
kiss I turned from last
night, a road I feared
to walk, sending
you home, the freeway

disappearing road,
taillights winking out,
my face pressed
to the door, lock
turned under fingers, I
stayed there a long time

Waking alone your touch
still shivers through
me, cold like glass
in my hand, lips
pressed to yours,
I drink.

New Year

1

      come midnight
I was lapping at your vulva

you raised your head from pillow
to announce the hour
      an arbitrary marker
           insignificant

for me the year turned on the moment
      you'd explode and dance
           beneath my tongue

body dissolved
      re-formed

your cries
      like chimes

2

      if only
all the loss could drain away
      at midnight

memory purged
    of dancing
          just one year ago
              blues band in Monterey
                  dancing despite
                      a light rain

    the new year chimes
her face dissolves
re-forming
    into yours

3

    so how to trust
this unformed year
birthed now
    in an unfamiliar room

we spin a dance
    of beginning
past made insignificant
    by touch and tongue

but could it be that seeds of ending
    are planted when we least suspect
      hope dissolving
          in a chime of rain
      in any midnight

Untrust

In your dream, I've been unfaithful, black sheets
streaked with evidence. It's like some scary
movie you can't stop watching, projected
in an endless loop. The co-star: my old
lover; no matter she no longer speaks
to me, that sex between us shrivelled to
an unshed tear. Your body turns, a slammed
door. "And I'd fucked you so hard," you mourn.

Morning floods the room where I lie naked
and suspect, but you don't see. My kisses
curdle on your neck, damp thighs such feeble
proof. If I could break into your brain I'd
rip film from sprocket; instead stand blinking,
blind in daylight, outside the locked theater.

Idolatry

"Always" is a false god before which we
kneel, tremble. "Forever" the hosannah
worrying hands and tongue. We pray for time
to cease its ceaseless unfolding, hold us
suspended in a safe pocket, our breath
warm against flannel, fingers curling lint.

Scarlet altar clothes are lined with golden
rings, unbroken circles with no escape
clause, dark cathedral echoes chanted vows.
We worship this hedge against the scrape of change,
as if future could be hammered into
place, the pattern fixed, contentment guaranteed.

As if the lungs could hold breath captive, or
devotion keep you always here with me.

Super Lotto

"That guy thinks
we're lottery dunces,"
you say of the hulking clerk
who jerks his head
in the direction of the kiosk
at Bob's Liquor Store.
He's out of Central Casting:
belly blubbered over belt,
sweat-stained tee, chin
grizzled with a few days'
growth of beard.

He's right—I've never
played before, just Scratchers
on a whim. I never win;
I have no luck. You've got
steadfast intention, strength
to summon what you want.
Like me—you waited seven
years for my relationship
to crumble; there to catch
me when I tumbled; one's
disaster is another's opportunity.

Now we gamble our desires:
you'll travel when you hit
the jackpot—Hawaii,
Fiji, Mexico—quit
your job and go. I dream
you'll be the one to see
in me the Grand Prize
and feel lucky, the one
who won't leave. That's
my prayer as we blacken

numbers in their tiny
squares. No system
for selecting, just
instinct life has taught
us to suspect. Which
of us has faith enough
to be a winner? We slap
our dollars bills before
the scowling clerk,
and so link fates.

to my reluctant valentine

the heart is a tough muscle. it pushes
blood around the body like a playground
bully, yanking down panties of little
girls, exposing tender parts. serves time in
reform school but returns unchanged, blistered
fist that hammers its cage of ribs. hardened
convict without remorse. someday will break
out, smash through bone, leave veins dangling, red
sea pooling in empty cavity. skulk
back streets, disguised, acquire new fingerprints,
never be taken alive. till then, pulses
alone in its watery sac, counts days
to release. all night dreams broken by songs
of the whispering lungs who keen: *no pardon.*

Bankrupt

"I feel romantically bankrupt"
        —A.C.

She tells me she spent it all, and more,
every dime and nickel that once nestled
safe in that porcelain belly.
How those coins must have clinked
slipped in through the thin slot
of the spine, how their tune
would have altered, grown duller
as wealth accumulated. And the spill
of them as they poured out in a rush—
wish I'd caught that shower.
Now she shows me a handful of smashed shards,
a pink-glazed ear, a corkscrew tail,
promises: *there's no more.* Poor piggy.

Clay slivers splinter her palms,
yet I feel flush with her—the fertile earth
of her eyes, her generous body.
I want to be a magician, pull a bright silver
dollar from behind the curve of her ear.
But her treasures are hoarded now,
vault so deep underground she's lost
the combination. Her hands
still bear the bruise of those prodigal coins;
she fingers the lint of empty pockets
as if they were the chambers of her heart.

Fetish

Bruise on my ass where you bit hard
skin purpled the shape of your mouth
still marks the pearled moon I view in mirror
like a flag planted in a colonized orb

Skin purpled, shock of your greedy mouth
set loose the body's rumbling tide
grateful to be colonized, pulled into orbit
after drifting so long in deep space

Borne on the body's shuddering tide
I wear these marks like jewels
no longer hidden in shadows of deep space
I want to gleam with emeralds, amethysts

I wear these marks like precious jewels
on my shoulder, neck, my collarbone
guard them like rare emeralds, amethysts
but still want everyone to see and envy

Shoulder, neck, hip, collarbone
tokens that remain when you've gone
if everyone could see, how they would envy
the depths at which you've touched me

I search for tokens when you've gone—
thumbprint on my thigh, vermillion nipple
conceal the depths at which you've touched me
the splayed viscera that seeks your entry

Thumbprint on thigh, vermillion nipple
I see them with my nerve-endings;
my splayed viscera wills your entry
flesh requires opening, transgression

My vision now resides in nerve-endings
and so I stroke the mark on pearled moon
flesh pleads for opening, transgression
bruise on my ass where you bit hard.

Maria's Lament

Always there's one little girl
who thinks she's different
from the rest, so when elders
warn against the monster,
forbid her to go near,
she disobeys, believes
she knows that lumbering
bully, has eyes to see
what has escaped the narrow
gaze of others—a tender
side, fissured pain in his red
eyes, clumsy longing
to be loved, thus made
unmonstrous.   She has strength,
she thinks, to love what's
been unloved. This makes her special,
will protect her. Is it a child's
simple faith or arrogance?
Only she can soften his stiff
spine, teach him the way
of flowers.   She takes his hand,
immense beside her own, fingers
swollen, bloodstained, dares
to touch the jagged scar that splits
his skull. He towers over her
but she trusts the power
of her smile.

    That same smile
will be twisted when they pull
her body from the lake, blue
cast to her skin, yellow hair
in soaked tendrils.
      And the fiend,
bereft, hunted, will howl
and stomp, eyes livid, mouth
torn in two, more monstrous
than he ever knew, clutching one
silk pale strand, one petal
crushed in a massive hand.

Body of Work

You say you hate
the waste of paper
from now on
you can scrawl
your poems across
my body

Find a nib fine
enough to skim
the surface of skin
shed its trail
of ink in every
curve and hollow

A pliant page
I'll drink your words
alphabet rising on jut
of bone, stretched against
flexed muscle, rubbed
raw with revision

Lash angry protest
poems along my spine
pen wistful childhood
odes behind my knees
tattoo love sonnets
on my neck and collarbone

Readers rendered breathless
by your fresh style
your productivity
will rocket, fevered
nights inscribing
metaphors like dreams

Charted on the pulp
of humble flesh
language sings
from your fingers
this folio croons
beneath your diction

Vampire

Let's say she really was a vampire.
It's more interesting
than the real story,
just another saga
of lesbian heartbreak—
seduction / rejection,
desire vanishing like the hem
of a black cape
at the first hint of morning.

Let's say I longed to lose
myself in her darkness,
retreat from the glare of day,
grow pale as mushrooms
in the moon's glow.
So when she warned me,
bared fangs and urged me to run,
I opened my white throat
and begged her suck.

I thought she would stay
if I let her change me.
She claimed I was danger—
daylight in my eyes, garlic on my tongue,
crucifix dangling at my hip.
I never dreamed I'd feel wind
as her wings sliced sky,
leaving me earthbound, drained,
cringing at the sun's kiss.

Poem for My 44th Birthday

Sasha wants to know
if it's the fear of aging
that made me weep on my 44th birthday
and for days after,
my friend Sasha who at 43
has already consulted
three plastic surgeons
about the face lift
she's saved for—ten grand!—
if I had ten grand
I would buy a house
to replace the one I can't
live in anymore since
my lover of nine years dumped
me for a woman of 34,
but it isn't crinkled
skin or deep creases
like parentheses around
my mouth or even
that I've fallen in love now
with someone who was barely
born when Kennedy
got shot—John not
Bobby—who insists we're
not in a relationship
though we talk everyday
on the phone and send
emails every night and go
out on the weekends and used
to make love before she pulled
the plug, I'm reduced
to a state of teenaged longing
and anxiety, wondering
will she call, will she say
"I love you" today or only
"talk to you later" and even

on this vague promise
I suspend myself, old
enough to know better
than to join this dance—
don't need *another* house
I can't live in—but I love
to dance with her, out
in the bars with the 20
year olds, the short skirts
I wear to entice her hands
to stroke the skin of my bare
thighs and I'm sleeping
in her bed the night
of my birthday after
a sweet day of sun and easy
music my body ticking
like a time bomb
that wants to go off but
we're not in a relationship
so she won't kiss me
but still presses close, head
on my shoulder, hip
curved like a comma beside
mine, I will myself awake
to savor it, my birthday
treat, not knowing when I might
have even this again, still
as night grays into morning
I slip inside a dream, chased
through twisting corridors
of public buildings, stairwells
and foyers, impersonal
houses, the killer close
behind, hands raised, five
bright colored birthday
candles in place of fingers,

they stretch toward me,
unlit, and if he touches
me, I'm dead, but I wake
too early, pillow pressed
between her body and mine,
this pliant barrier, my
eyes flood, this new morning
of my 45th year.

Biographical Note

TERRY WOLVERTON is the author of *Bailey's Beads,* a novel and *Black Slip,* a collection of poetry. Her fiction, poetry, essays and drama have been published in periodicals internationally, including *Glimmer Train Stories, Zyzzyva, Many Mountains Moving,* and *The Jacaranda Review,* and widely anthologized. She is currently working on a memoir, *Insurgent Muse,* for City Lights Books, and a novel-in-poems, *Embers.*

She has also edited twelve literary anthologies, including *His: brilliant new fiction by gay men* and *Hers: brilliant new fiction by lesbians,* volumes 1, 2, and 3, and the upcoming *Lesbian Fiction At the Millennium* and *Gay Fiction At the Millennium.*

In 1997, she founded Writers at Work, a center for creative writing in Los Angeles, where she teaches several weekly workshops in fiction and poetry.